Google Classroom 2020

The Complete Step by Step Illustrated Guide to Learn Everything You Need to Know About Google Classroom

By

Henry Class

Copywrite Notice:

—

Table of Contents

Introduction

Google classroom is going to change the essence of instruction. For quite a long time, teachers have spent such an extensive amount their time both inside and outside the classroom, attempting to locate the most ideal approach to instruct their students and give input immediately.

These set aside a long effort to achieve and could cut into the learning time for the students. Now and again, to save time, teachers would pick the most effortless alternatives for picking up, removing inventiveness and a portion of the fun in learning.

The headship was not only for the teacher. Students frequently needed to monitor papers from various classes and in the messiness, they may pass up significant information about the assignments.

Google Classroom is a free platform that can improve instruction for both the student and the teacher. Teachers can have every one of their classes in a single spot, dole out schoolwork and send information and save a ton of time. Students can generally be forward-thinking on their work, receive input on their assignments, and even arrive at their teacher continuously. It is a success win for the two both the students and the teachers and can make learning fun and charming once more.

This guide will give you the information you need to begin with Google Classroom.

We begin this guide with some fundamental information on Google classroom, the benefits, features and afterward move into the various errands that teachers can do and a portion of the various assignments that students can likewise exploit. Wrapping up with probably the best tips of how to utilize classroom. This guide will assist you with seeing all the extraordinary Google Classroom highlights and begin on utilizing this application for your benefits.

With all the alternatives for educational platforms accessible to utilize, Google Classroom is standing out with simple applications that numerous as of now appreciate what not the accessible highlights that you can use for free.

Check out this guide now and learn exactly how astonishing this platform can be.

Chapter 1

What is Google Classroom?

Google Classroom is a free online stage that assists with overseeing arranging, assets, assignments, and correspondence among yourself and your class. If your school, doesn't have one as of now, you'll have to pursue a Google Applications for Instruction account to utilize Google Classroom which will give all of you the Google Applications administrations including Drive, Docs, Sheets, Gmail and Calendar. Google Classroom is accessible on tablets, telephones, and desktops, making it versatile for both instructors and students.

Google Classroom assists with keeping your computerized classroom sorted out. It sits on Google Drive and makes envelopes for you for each class and every task to keep yourself and your understudies sorted out. Both yourself and students can attach documents to the classroom from your Google Drive and all files moved through Google Classroom are consequently stored in Google Drive.

Both teachers and students can monitor all assignments that are expected and teachers can see who has finished their work and give feedback in real-time to students. Student work can be resubmitted and evaluated as well, whenever required.

In nutshell, Google Classroom is a free web administration created by Google for schools that plans to streamline making, circulating, and evaluating assignments. One of the basic roles of Google Classroom is to smooth out the way toward sharing files both for instructors and students.

Google Classroom incorporates docs, sheets, Slides, Gmail, and schedule into a firm stage to oversee student and instructor correspondence. Students can join any of the class using a private code that will be provided by the teacher.

Instructors can make, appropriate, and mark assignments all inside the Google ecosystem. Each class makes a different organizer in a particular folder, where the student can submit work to be evaluated by an instructor.

Most of the assignments which include the set-dates & time are added to google calendar, and also each assignment can also belong to a particular set of categories or topics.

Instructors can screen the advancement for every student by evaluating the modification history of a file, and in the wake of being reviewed, educators can return work alongside remarks.

The classroom has versatile applications, accessible for iOS and Android.

In this guide, you will become familiar with Google Classroom and take your skill to a higher level. This guide will give you all that you have to begin utilizing Google Classroom and best practices to assist you with taking advantage of this tool.

Ideal for a tenderfoot to moderate expertise levels! Consider this your best guide for Google Classroom!

Thanks for investing in this book. I'm sure you will enjoy reading this guide. If you find this book useful and want to encourage me to produce more guides like this, kindly leave an honest review on Amazon.

Chapter 2

Google Classroom Basics

We have 4 main tabs at the top and they are Stream, Classwork, People, and Grades.

The Classwork Tab

In this section, you can easily do many tasks such as creating a mission, creating a subject, adding materials, asking of questions, and reuse of previous posts.

Do you Create an assignment?

Click on the plus sign and select Create Assignment. Additionally, you may specify a topic to the assignment should you require.

How to Make a topic

If you will need to arrange the assignments/questions, create several topics. Just click on the plus sign and select Create Topic.

You will just need to click on the + sign and then select 'materials. This permits you to add all of the materials to the classwork tab and then arrange them according to various topics.

Click on the plus sign and select Create Query.

The People Tab

This particular tab is all about adding and removing teachers or students from the course.

Visit: www.classroom.google.com, then click on the + sign and then select 'Join Class'. Then they will have to insert the course code (find under Individuals). Or you could invite yourself by typing their names and emails on the search box or through the class private code.

When it's necessary you can leave a course for a co-teacher. If you leave a course you co-teach, you cannot open it unless re-invited.

Stream Tab

This section is similar to the feed social media (Facebook, Instagram).

How to Make a post/announcement

Have you got something important to say? Create a Post or Reuse Post (it is possible to reuse a post that you have used before). In this section, you can add an image, video, document, file, or link to your article.

Grades Tab

I don't use this tab for kindergarten pupils.

Settings section

In this section, you can easily change the title of your class.

i.   There's no save button since changes are saved automatically.

ii.   If you would like any of the packets in the Google Slides to be interactive (drag and touch attribute), you and pupils should just open it in 'edit mode'

iii. You can now see the class code right on the Stream Tab, at the top banner or class picture.

iv. In case you've got similar grades/classes, simply copy an existing course with all the missions and then make adjustments.

v. Use Archive a Class attribute rather than deleting. This way you'll be able to bring back an archived class if you would like to use it later. If not, you can go ahead to delete a course.

Advantages of Google Classroom

Easy to set up

Teachers can directly add students or even share a private code so their class can join. Google Classroom doesn't take time. It takes just minutes just to set up.

Saves your time

The paperless assignment work-flow which makes life easier. So in one easy place, teachers can create, review, and also mark assignments quickly.

Improving organization

Students can see all of their assignments on an assignment page, while all class materials (e.g. documents, photos, and videos) are automatically filed into folders in Google Drive.

Enhances communication

Google Classroom allows teachers to send announcements and start class discussions instantly. Students can share resources or provide answers to questions on the stream.

Affordable and secure

Like the rest of G Suite for Education services, Google Classroom contains no ads, never uses your content or student data for advertising purposes, and is free.

Permissions note

Camera: Needed to allow the user to take photos or videos and post them to Google Classroom.

Microphone: Needed to enable audio capture for recording videos to be posted to the Classroom.

Photos: Needed to allow the user to attach photos or videos to Google Classroom. Photos or videos posted to the Classroom will be stored on Google servers to show them in the Classroom.

Chapter 3

Google Classroom Features

Under the Classroom app, students and teachers have access to features that are not found in personal Google accounts. For example, in Forms, teachers can add images to questions or as multiple-choice answers.

Inbox by Gmail has Google Classroom messages grouped in Inbox, making it easy for teachers and students to find important updates and highlights. Also, the Classroom tool lets teachers organize the class stream by adding topics to posts, and teachers and students can filter the stream for specific topics.

Google Classroom also encourages parent participation. Teachers can invite parents to the Google Classroom to share summaries of student work and to receive automated email summaries of student work and class announcements.

A summary of Google Classroom features includes the following:

- ✓ Connects instructors with students.
- ✓ It makes it easy to create a class and invite learners.
- ✓ Helps instructors to distribute assignments.
- ✓ Facilitates communications between instructors and students.
- ✓ Allows teachers to create, review, and mark assignments.

✓ Allows students to see assignments on assignments, documents, and class materials in one place.

This core products are so valuable which make-up the Google-for-Education suite which includes Google Gmail account, Google Classroom, Google Drive, Google Calendar, Google Vault, Google Docs, Google Sheets, Google Forms, Google Slides, Google Sites, and Google Hangouts.

Unlike the Individual Google Accounts, the Google Classroom tool is available only to instructors and learners, the apps are offered free of charge, and support is also provided for free.

Chapter 4

The Benefits of Google
Classroom to Teachers, Students and Parents

Google Classroom gives the various unmistakable advantage to teachers, but at the same time, it's significant to college students and even designers.

As of late, paperless classrooms have gotten more typical than any other time in recent memory. Indeed, even in rustic territories and at universities, students currently complete most of their work on the web. This change spares a cost for the earth by reducing paper use, and it's likewise helpful for students, particularly the individuals who probably won't approach a real classroom however go virtually.

Google Classroom was released in the late spring of 2014 and is currently utilized in classrooms around the US. There are numerous advantages to using this free tool.

Communication and Collaborate

The in-built tool makes speaking with students and guardians a breeze. Teachers and students can send messages, post to the stream, send private remarks on assignments, and give criticism on work. Teachers have full authority over student remarks and posts. They can likewise speak with guardians through individual messages or through Classroom email announcements which incorporate class declarations and due dates.

The classroom offers a few different ways for students to work together. Teachers can encourage online conversations among students and create group work inside the Classroom. What's more, students can work together on Google Docs which have been shared by the teacher.

Coordinate It with Other Google Items

Google Classroom likewise coordinates effectively with Google Docs, Sheets, and Slides. For schools on a limited financial plan, offering a platform that matches up with other free tools gives an approach to schools and students to come into the twentieth century without spending a fortune on costly classroom programming.

Teachers give assignments, and students consider those to be a task. When the work is done, the student confirms it. An organized arrangement of steps for task culmination keeps everybody composed and stays away from disarray about which tasks are expected.

Engagement and Differentiation

Most digital natives are OK with innovation and will be increasingly well-suited to take proprietorship in their learning through the utilization of innovation. The classroom offers various approaches to make learning intuitive and synergistic. It offers teachers the capacity to separate assignments, incorporate videos and site pages into videos, and make synergistic gathering assignments.

Through Classroom, teachers are effectively ready to separate instruction for students. Allocating exercises to the entire class, singular students, or gatherings of students makes only a couple of basic steps while making a task on the Classwork page.

Feedback and Data Analysis

Giving significant input to students is an important piece of all learning. Inside the reviewing tool of the Classroom, teachers can send input to every student on assignments. The capacity to make a remark bank for some time later is additionally accessible inside the reviewing apparatus. What's more, the Classroom portable application permits clients to clarify work.

To make learning important, teachers ought to break down information from evaluations to guarantee students are understanding learning objectives. Information from evaluations can undoubtedly be sent out into Sheets for arranging and investigation.

Exploit a Simple to-Utilize tool

Google Classroom offers a profoundly natural and overly simple-to-learn interface. The platform takes you through each progression of the procedure. At the point when you land on the main page of your classroom, you'll be welcome to "communicate with your group here." You can make announcements and schedule them to go out individually. You can likewise react to any student notes. The interface is plain as well, which implies there's no learning curve to utilizing the product.

Permit Students to Interface with Different Students

One component of Google Classroom is making assignments, for example, questions. You can set up what number of focuses an inquiry is worth and even permit students to associate with each other. A simple to-get to gathering encourages collaboration, even in an online environment, and empowers students to gain from each other.

Notwithstanding the students interfacing with each other, the teacher can associate with singular students and even with guardians through email, presents on a stream, private remarks and criticism. You can likewise make a class declaration that applies to all the students enlisted.

Learn to Use an Online Classroom Platform

Several universities have recently used a combination of physical appearance and online classroom environments. This is a huge benefit as using Google Classroom helps you to experience an online environment as either as a teacher or a student.

As a teacher, you can also login in as a student and see out how the platform works so that you can know how to guide any confused students. This is a new level of learning, as the world increasing in technology, expects even more online courses, even for topics such as web designing, where students can now learn a lesson online and upload his or her work via a whiteboard or even as an attachment.

Accessibility and Time Saver

Google Classroom can be gotten from any PC employing Google Chrome or from any cell phone. All files transferred by teachers and students are uploaded in a Classroom folder on Google Drive. Clients can get to the Classroom whenever, anyplace. Students no longer need to stress over smashed PCs or hungry mutts.

Google Classroom is a huge time saver. With all the different resources compressed in one place which gives you the ability to access the Classroom anywhere, there will be more free-time for teachers to complete any other tasks. Since everyone can access the Classroom from a mobile device, teachers and students can participate through their phones or tablets.

Then for students, all their resources for a class can be found in one single place. So, there's no need to find a book, grab a notebook, rush to the classroom for a lecture, or to print out an essay. Instead, the class lessons can be viewed online, reply to questions, and even submit work all in one place. The interface stays neat and organized so there will be no need wasting time looking for that lost classroom materials.

For teachers, all of the students, information, submissions, and grades are in one convenient location.

Stops the Excuses

A few students appear to ceaselessly have an excuse for not turning in their work. You've heard the old "the dog ate my schoolwork" answer, yet a few students take reasons to another level. With an advanced classroom, work is relegated and submitted web-based, which means it can't be "lost." Online platforms additionally permit guardians to keep steady over what their student finished what despite everything needs wrapping up.

A few schools are likewise using web-based learning on snow days as opposed to compelling students to make up scratch-offs because of extraordinary climate. Never again is spring break cut into or school in meeting for seven days after it ought to have finished. Rather, the school gives access to web-based learning modules so work proceeds even on days when school doesn't.

The Future is here

Google is on the front line of innovation and what individuals look for from online frameworks. An online classroom framework permits schools and individuals who simply need to offer information to others a spot to do as such without going through a great deal of cash. The free efficiency tools likewise give you a spot to keep classes sorted out and store reports.

Google Classroom smoothed out the whole instruction process by dispensing with the need to print and duplicate papers and physically enter grades into an evaluation book. Rather, everything is done carefully, sparing time, and exertion. Teachers additionally save time and can concentrate on individualized learning.

Chapter 5

Setting up your Google Classroom

1. **Go to: www.classroom.google.com.**

   ✓ Google Classroom is currently accessible for Google Education accounts just like your normal Gmail email accounts. If you have a Google email account, then you can now be able to utilize Google Classroom.

2. **Click on the "+" button in the top upper right to set up your first class.**

   (It's close to the checkerboard symbol you use to get to the entirety of your applications.) At that point click "Create class."

   ✓ If you're just a beginner then your screen will probably resemble the one above.

   ✓ If you have a few classes as of now, they'll show on this home screen. You can include new classes with the "+" button.

3. **Include information about your class.**

   ✓ You must include a name for your class. This is how your students will recognize your class when they open Google Classroom.

   ✓ Use the "section" field to separate between various classes of a similar sort. Numerous teachers will utilize this field for the class time frame. (This field is discretionary.)

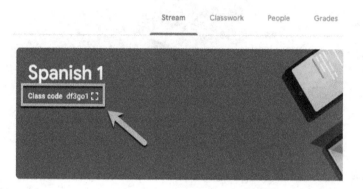

4. When your class is made, students can begin joining it.

✓ Students can get in your class with a special join code. This is a speedy, simple approach to get students into your group. By showing the join code, students can sign in to Google Classroom, click the "+" button, and "Join class" so you can enter the join code. At that point, they're added to your group.

✓ You can also invite students to your class group by email. This is a decent alternative if students don't meet face to face for your class. To do this, click the "Individuals" tab at the top. At that point, click the "Welcome Students" button (a symbol with an individual and an or more). You can invite students separately with email addresses or by groups if all students are in Google groups.

5. Alter your Google Classroom.

✓ There won't be any students in your class the second you make it. This is an ideal opportunity to get imaginative and have a ton of fun with it! Click "Select Theme" on the right corner side of the header. It will open a display gallery of header pictures you can use to flavor up your classroom.

✓ You can likewise transfer images to show at the highest point of your Classroom. You can utilize a picture of your class or something that relates to your class. A few teachers will make a custom header picture with significant information and fun graphics.

Communicate with your class here

Chapter 6

Using Google Classroom in everyday class

A fter your class is set up and students go along with, you have a completely working Google Classroom. Congrats!

In any case, you would prefer not to stop there.

Here are a few things you can do in your Classroom:

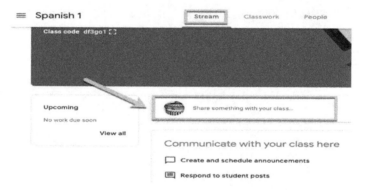

1. Include an announcement.

Announcements are presented on the class stream, however, there isn't an evaluation related to them.

Head to class Stream and click on the "share something with your class". You can then add the content for your announcement. And add any files

(Which you can attach or from Google Drive), any YouTube videos, or any links you'd like. Then post it (or you can schedule it to send later).

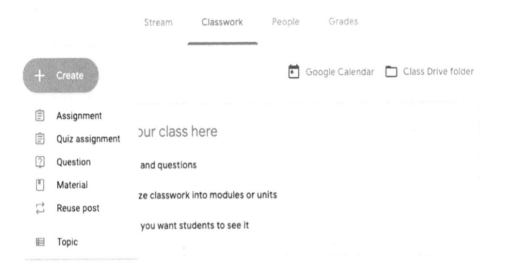

1. **You can create a quiz, assignment, task, attach material, or even reuse an old post.**

   This is the place students get the opportunity to work! You can make an evaluated (or ungraded) question for students to reply, a quiz, OR a task for students to do. You can make them under the "Classwork" tab (above). You can likewise add material you need the students to make use of or they can reuse an old post.

Things to add on your task or question (above):

✓ An illustrative title for your task. (Expert tip: It's acceptable to number your assignments to dispose of disarray.)

✓ A description. This is useful for students who were missing and for alluding back to a past task later.

✓ The points. Pick what number of points the task/question is worth (or utilize the drop-down menu to make it ungraded).

✓ A due date. Pick when the task is expected (or don't utilize a due date).

✓ A topic. (this is also another important area)

✓ Attaching a file. Attaching files include files from Google Drive, incorporate YouTube videos gives students a connection.

Relegate the task promptly, plan it to post naturally later, or save your task as a draft to complete later.

2. Organize your class with topics.

If you have various sections, units, subjects, and so forth inside your class, you can classify your assignments and inquiries by point to keep everything sorted out.

Under "Classwork", click the "Create" button and include a topic. At that point, at whatever you create another task or assignment, you'll have the option to add that subject to it.

3. Grade and return work.

When students have finished work, you can give criticism and grade the task. Click on the "Classwork" button and click on the task to see student work.

Here are some of the moves you can make:

1. Find the task by students who have handed the work over or all students who were given the task. (Simply click on the huge number.) Or, you can sort by different choices with the drop-down menu below the huge numbers.)

2. Open and see student work by tapping on it. Inside student documents, slide presentations, and so on., you can add your comment to the file.

3. Type and see private comments to the student by tapping on the student's name. You can likewise observe when files were turned in with the history.

4. Add an evaluation to student work.

5. When you're completely done, return work to students. Be certain you've checked the crate close to their names and snap the "Arrival" button.

Chapter 7

Using Google Classroom to Train Your Employees

Proficient turn of events and employment-related training can be a wellspring of hopelessness for some individuals. In any case, consider the possibility that employers could break that shape by making training fun, intelligent, and paramount. Google Classroom breathes life into that chance. Utilizing the numerous assets Classroom brings to the table can extend representative information and offer various open doors for development.

East to Set Up a Classroom & Invite the Students

Before training can start, a Google Classroom must be set up for representatives. Make sure to give the classroom a suitable, explicit title that associates with your requirements. Separate classrooms might be set up for various subjects; in any case, the most effective strategy is to set up one classroom which isolates themes into learning modules. Remember to invite workers to become students in the class or offer the classroom join code.

Make a Training Module

The most significant part of utilizing the Classroom as a professional improvement tool is organization. Setting up the Classroom with training topics (additionally alluded to as modules) can save employers time and keep employees locked in. When the essential arrangement of the classroom is finished, it's an ideal opportunity to make training modules. On the Classwork tab, click the +sign to make another theme and name it as indicated by the substance of the training. For instance, the classroom beneath is titled Professional Development & Training with a training subject of " Differentiated Instruction" which will fill in as the primary module.

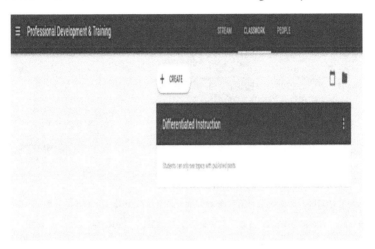

Adding Content to Your Module

There are a few alternatives for adding content to a module in the Classroom. Including assignments or questions is a simple errand, yet making connecting with content is the place the Classroom has an advantage. Including an inquiry is a snappy method to get employees occupied with a professional exchange.

While including a task, users have the choice to include files and other content from Google Drive, for example, Slides or forms. YouTube recordings or links can likewise be added to assignments. This gives chances to make content which associates with various taking in styles and keeps employees from packing into a space for "sit and get" professional advancement meetings. Setting a course of events for finishing permits students the adaptability to take part in activities at their own pace individually.

Evaluating Learning

Assessing learning is a significant segment of professional turn of events. Classroom gives different tools to make assessments a breeze for employers. While making an inquiry, there is a choice to make the inquiry open-finished for client reactions or to settle on its numerous decisions. What's more, users can transfer a Google Form for a progressively point by point appraisal of learning. This is additionally an effective strategy for social event input about the training itself and whether the employer needs to make changes or acclimation to the module.

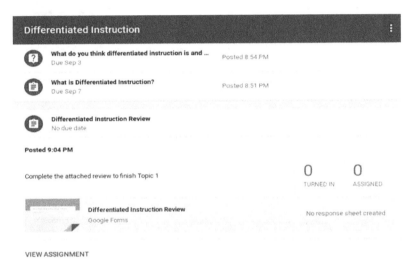

Following Up

Follow up is one of the most significant parts of the professional turn of events. Making a subsequent conversation permits employees to give criticism on the usage of content scholarly. It additionally gives a gathering to talk about zones where help is required and permits friends to give direction to each other.

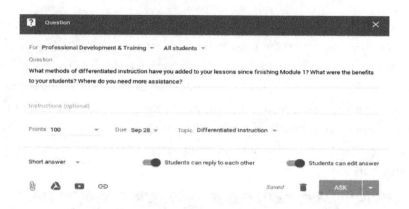

Chapter 8

Things you can't do with Google Classroom

There are a couple of things you should know before you begin utilizing Google Classroom for an inappropriate reason. It's a web-based learning platform, yet it isn't:

A Chatbox Function: You can comment on assignments and announcements, yet there's no chat section. Although if you would like to be in direct contact with your students, you can send them an email, or you can enable other Google applications to assume control over that work. Such as Hangouts Meet.

Using a Quiz or Test tool: There are a few prospects with regards to making a quiz in Google Classroom, yet it's still not intended to be a test tool all alone. There are such huge numbers of other great applications for that. Consider Google Forms or BookWidgets quiz tools.

#1 Option: You can include tests and assignments from other educational applications directly inside Google Classroom, for instance, a BookWidgets test that gets automatically graded.

#2 Option: This is what you can do inside Google Classroom itself: Include questions. At that point pick between an open answer or a various question. Not unreasonably amazing, I know. It's advised you pick the first option.

A Conversation Gathering: This is known as a discussion forum. You can make announcements, and students can truly comment on them, however, it is anything but an incredible fit for conversations. Look at Padlet in case you're searching for a straightforward yet successful, free classroom tool that engages conversations (and other cool things).

Chapter 9

Google Classroom App on Google Play Store

Google Classroom is a free joint effort tool for teachers and students. Teachers can make an online classroom, welcome students to the class at that point make and disseminate assignments. Inside the Google Classroom, students and teachers can have discussions about the assignments, and teachers can follow the student's advancement. Schools must enroll for a free Google Applications for Instruction record to utilize Classroom.

The Google Classroom begins as a platform administration for schools, non-benefit organizations and anybody with an individual Google slides account. Google Classroom makes it simple for students and teachers to interface – inside and outside of schools. It assists saves with timing and physical paper, and furthermore makes it simple to set up classes, circulate a task, convey among individual students and teachers and furthermore remain sorted out.

The Google Classroom can also help teachers to fix, collect and mark assignments paperless without a physical presence, it also includes time-saving features such as the ability to automatically make a copy of a Google document for each of the student. Google Classroom also creates Drive folders for each assignment and for each student to help keep everyone organized.

Students can monitor what's expected on the Assignments page and start working with only a tick. Teachers can rapidly observe who has or hasn't finished the work, and give immediate, ongoing criticism and stamps legitimately in Google Classroom.

With the versatile application for iOS, students and teachers can see their classes and speak with their schoolmates continuously. Students can open their assignments and work on them legitimately utilizing their iPhone or iPad. Teachers can monitor who has turned in work and imprint the task – at school or in a hurry. Students and teachers get notices when they have new content in Google Classroom, so they are consistently state-of-the-art.

Chapter 10

List of top Chrome Extensions for Both Teachers and Students

The greater part of the advanced student work is done inside an internet browser. On the off chance that you are in school or college, odds are a large portion of your work and examining is additionally done in the program.

In this segment, I will manage you through the absolute best Chrome extensions each student must-have. A portion of these will assist you with getting progressively gainful; some will assist you with forestalling botches in your composition.

These Google Chrome extensions are allowed to introduce, and the applications are excessively simple to utilize.

GRAMMAR & SPELLING TOOLS

GRAMMARLY

M

A Better Way to Write

It may happen that we need

to decide tomorrow.

Rewrite the phrase

We may need

Grammarly is a propelled language checking tool that tests your composition against several linguistic mix-ups.

The free form of this application will assist you with forestalling linguistic slip-ups in the vast majority of your composition. Another exceptional thing about this extension is that it chips away at a large number of the sites which incorporates Google Gmail Record, Google Doc and some more. It can't be contrast with most other sentence structure tools, since it gives the choice for you to choose which English you compose — regardless of whether American or English.

The exceptional variant of this application won't just assist you with checking for language structure botches however it will likewise assist you with checking your content against counterfeiting. It additionally causes you set a pace for your composition and proposes alterations as needs be.

LANGUAGE TOOL

Language tool chrome extension

Despite the fact that Chrome's worked in spellchecker can assist you with fixing some spelling botches, it is worked to assist you with checking and fix syntactic mistakes. LanguageTool will assist you with comprehending sentence structure mistakes in excess of 20 distinct dialects.

This tool chips away at a few sites both via web-based networking media and furthermore on email inboxes. LanguageTool serves to underlines any content that needs adjustment and furthermore permits you to comprehend any syntactic mistake with only a tick. It assists with stamping in content with spelling botches and furthermore fix linguistic mistakes.

GRAMMARBASE

GrammarBase is a free sentence structure checking tool that checks for everything from Accentuation to Style. It can assist you with fixing syntactic mistakes in your composition with only a single tick. It likewise checks your content against literary theft.

The best part about this syntax checker is that it is totally free and doesn't require any moves up to open more highlights. It deals with practically all sites including Gmail and Facebook.

GINGER

Ginger is one of the most well-known syntax checking tools on the Web. It permits you to fix sentence structure botches with only a tick. It likewise causes you get recommendations for clearness and rethinking sentences.

With this tool, you can without much of a stretch interpret the content with a single tick. With the free form, you can fix practically all basic sentence structure botches in your composition and records over the web. This tool with Reddit, Facebook, Gmail, Google Docs and practically even some different destinations.

PLAGIARISM CHECKERS

PROWRITINGAID

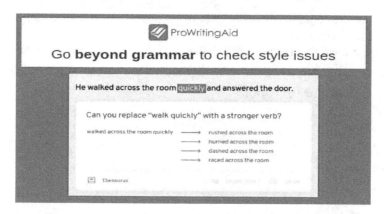

ProWritingAid is a free tool that checks your composition for sentence structure slip-ups and offers proposals to improve your composing style. It can assist you with forestalling missteps and make your composing more grounded. It additionally accompanies a written falsification checker.

It takes a shot at practically all sites over the web including email inboxes, Twitter, and other famous locales. It accompanies an implicit Thesaurus that offers proposals to improve your composition.

All the proposals can be applied with only a single tick directly from the content as this extension will feature the content consequently that needs revision or improvement.

PLAGLY

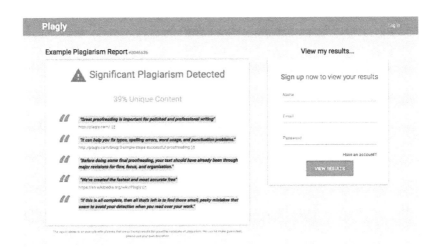

Plagly is a language checker and written falsification checker. It checks your content against a huge number of pages on the web and reports stealing entries in your content. It likewise offers proposals to fix language structure mistakes in your composition.

In spite of the fact that the initial hardly any activities are free, you have to pay a moderate month to month expense to get full access to the tool and boundless copyright infringement checking.

PLAGIARISM CHECKER

Art of writing

Writing is an art and it needs to be perfected with practice and once you do tha various doors of success for yourself. So, let's get started and tell you how you

Literary theft Checker is a free chrome extension that checks the content for counterfeiting. You can choose any section and right-click the determination to check it for originality.

It is totally free and doesn't expect you to pay to get full access. Despite the fact that it's not the ideal tool to check originality with, it is totally free and offers essential written falsification checking.

MYBIB

MyBB is a free reference generator extension for Google Chrome. This chrome extension prompts you on whether a source is believable. It will assist you with generating references dependent on in excess of 9000 upheld, pre-characterized reference styles which incorporates APA, AMA, MLA, Harvard and Chicago.

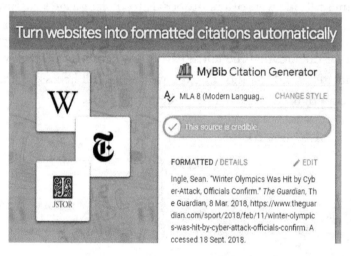

You can either duplicate your book reference to the clipboard or download it as a Word record. It can do what EasyBib and Refer to This for Me improve. This is my suggested tool.

CITE THIS FOR ME

1-click website referencing in APA, Chicago, MLA, or Harvard style

Cite This For Me naturally makes site references and referencing in reports with a wide range of styles to look over. The styles incorporate Chicago, APA, MLA, and Harvard.

It does everything with only a tick of a catch. It permits you to make lovely references that look great and are adequate for scholarly use.

EASYBIB

Cite credible sources with our extension.

EasyBib is a free Chrome extension that refers to sites with a single tick and it additionally informs you on the validity concerning the sites you are referring to. It is vastly improved to depend on EasyBib than a theory all alone.

It can inform you which references are acceptable and can be utilized and the one you ought to maintain a strategic distance from simply like a plague.

GOOGLE DICTIONARY

Google Dictionary Google's legitimate Chrome extension that permits you to see definitions straightforwardly from Google's authentic word reference. Not any more looking through words on Google to check their significance or spelling.

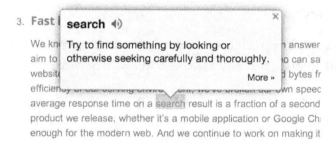

You can either tap the chrome extension symbol and type/glue the word you need Google to characterize. Or then again you can basically double tap a word anyplace on the page and this extension will show you the significance in a little in-line popup box.

POWER THESAURUS

Power Thesaurus is a free Chrome extension that can show you the antonyms and equivalents without leaving the page you found the word on. It can assist you with improving your composition by making it super-simple to discover comparable, all the more remarkable words to supplant your powerless words.

You can check the Thesaurus utilizing this extension by either choosing a word and right-tapping the choice. Or on the other hand you can tap the extension symbol in the menu bar to type the word physically and search the Thesaurus.

QUILLBOT

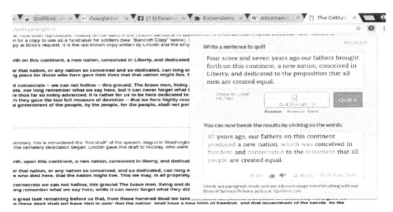

Quillbot is a free chrome extension that causes you supplant words with their choices from the Thesaurus with only a tick. Rather than discovering options for each word all alone, you can essentially place a passage or sentence in this tool and snap the Plume it catches to create another section with elective words.

STAY FOCUSED

In the event that you don't care for squandering hours via web-based networking media locales or even YouTube, at that point this application named 'Remain Centered' is the correct chrome extension you have been searching for. It helps square diverting sites by limiting 5-minute online networking registration which can transform into hours.

This extension permits you to set an everyday stipend limit for "internet-based life and diverting sites". It defaults to just 10 minutes. Your day by day remittance is the quantity of minutes you are permitted to peruse the locales in your interruption list.

On the off chance that you are a bad-to-the-bone profitability nerd, you can empower the atomic alternative from the settings which obstruct all the sites totally. The atomic choice can hinder all sites on the off chance that you need to invest energy disconnected dealing with troublesome stuff when you can't manage the cost of interruptions.

In the event that you need to peruse the Web openly on ends of the week or after work, you can modify the Dynamic Hours and Dynamic Days alternatives. You can enter all the locales you wish to obstruct in the interruptions list from the alternatives menu or you can tap the extension's symbol in the menu bar and add the present site to the rundown from that point.

EVERNOTE WEB CLIPPER

Evernote is the most mainstream note-taking application utilized by a large number of individuals around the globe. It can cause you increasingly beneficial as well as help you to recall all that you learn. The best part about utilizing Evernote is the capacity to catch notes from online content, for example, website pages, messages, and other content with only a tick.

Evernote's note-taking procedure can accelerate your work process and offer a simple method to store all that you learn.

Evernote Web Scissors permits you to catch nearly everything on the Web. From inquire about material to images, you can save everything to your Evernote account with only a couple of snaps.

This extension additionally permits you to take screen captures. The best part about this extension is that it permits you to catch just pieces of a page. In addition, it can assist you with choosing the contents of website pages like Tweets, Reddit Posts, Blog Entries and some more.

The great part for sparing content with the Internet Scissors is that you have a made sure about duplicate in your Evernote whether the page is on the web or has gone disconnected.

TODOIST

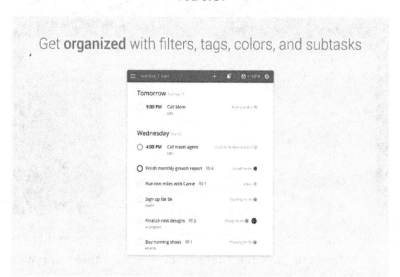

Todoist is one of the most famous lineups for the day applications. It offers applications for all gadgets including Android, iOS, and so forth. Keeping a lineup for the day in your mind will just injure your efficiency. The Todoist Chrome extension permits you to remain beneficial the entire day without overlooking any of your assignments. The spotless interface makes it simple to watch out for every one of your undertakings for the afternoon.

Todoist is made in light of coordinated effort. You can without much of a stretch work together with others who use Todoist on the undertakings and ventures. You can leave remarks on assignments for your schoolmates.

What I like the most about Todoist is that it naturally proposes you time and date for undertakings dependent on your calendar. At the point when you make an assignment, it will propose a date on the off chance that you click the calendar symbol close to the undertaking name.

To improve your work process, Todoist permits you to partition your errands with activities and marks. You can likewise make channels to channel errands dependent on needs, undertakings, and what their identity is alloted to. Todoist can be an insignificant plan for the day or an undeniable profitability machine with bunches of highlights, for example, Undertakings, Marks, Rehash, Updates, Channels, Names, and some more.

DUALLESS

Dualless encourages you work with two open windows one next to the other. Taking a shot at only one screen can be tiring a direct result of all the exchanging between different windows. On the off chance that you can't manage the cost of two screens, you can utilize Dualless to mastermind two windows next to each other with only a couple of snaps.

You can relocate windows next to each other yourself however this extension encourages you do it with only a couple of snaps. Dualless offers a wide range of design varieties to browse. You should simply choose two tabs you need to part and snap the extension's symbol to choose the window split design.

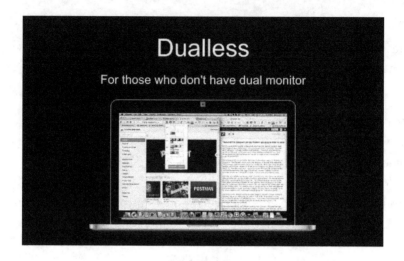

AUTO HIGHLIGHT

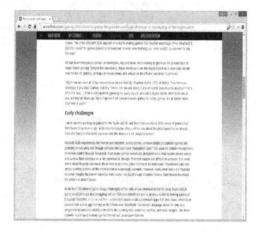

Auto Highlight empowers you read online content much speedier by means of normally including the most critical bits of the page. It is foolishly careful with the highlights usually. It can help you with cutting down your scrutinizing time down the center.

Instead of scrutinizing the whole article, you can tap the Auto Highlight image in the menu bar ensuing to presenting the extension and it will include areas in the content that are the most-huge. The extension highlights sections with a yellow establishment. You can adjust the concealing arrangement of the highlighted content from the extension decisions page.

KAMI EXTENSION

Kami is a free extension that permits you to alter and explain PDF archives directly in your program. It permits you to add content to archives or even draw on them. It works disconnected and accompanies many highlights for nothing.

You can alter archives from Google Drive, or Google Classroom. Kami is made to be utilized cooperatively among students and teachers. It encourages you team up with your teachers and different students without any problem.

Regardless of whether you need to clarify your notes to make them progressively decipherable or need to get your teacher's survey on a task, Kami can assist you with it. It offers a smooth work process for both explaining PDF archives and teaming up over them.

NIMBUS

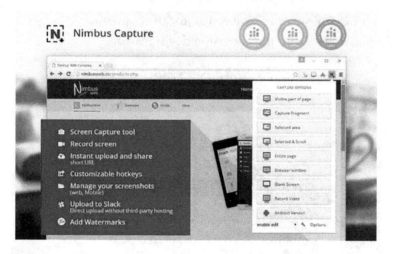

Radiance causes you catch screen captures and record screencasts of your program. It permits you to catch full page screen captures just as catch just chosen zones of the page. It additionally permits you to comment on and alter your screen captures directly in your program. You can likewise add your watermark marking to all your screen catches with only a couple of snaps.

It can assist you with editing your screen captures without leaving your program. It permits you to include embed watermarks, content, and pictures on your screen captures. You can likewise obscure pieces of the pictures with only a couple of snaps. Aura can assist you with catching significant information simply the manner in which it is shown on the page.

LASTPASS

Securely store passwords, notes, addresses and more, all in your vault

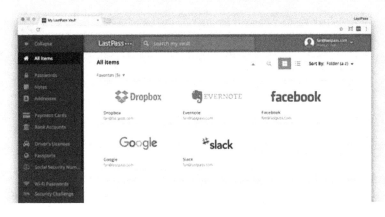

LastPass is extraordinary compared to other secret phrase supervisors that store your passwords safely in the cloud and gives you secure access to each site you login to from each PC and cell phone.

LastPass recollects every one of your passwords for you, so you don't need to pick frail or simple to recall passwords. It's something beyond a secret key supervisor. It can store passwords, yet additionally other significant information, for example, your charge card subtleties, your financial balance subtleties.

LastPass accompanies a free arrangement or you can move up to premium plans beginning at just $3 every month.

Thanks for investing in this book. I'm sure you are enjoying this guide so far. If you find this book useful and want to encourage me to produce more guide like this, kindly leave an honest review on Amazon

Chapter 11

The Effective Ways
to Use Google Classroom.

he most effective method to Add Students to a Class in Google Classroom

T   After you set up a class in Google Classroom, you will need to invite your students to the class.

You can invite the same number of students as you wish. You can either invite students from inside your class, or you can give students a code with which they can sign in to your class (which is surely the simpler approach!).

Invite students to your class

You can invite students from either the school's registry or from your own contacts or gathering list. Simply follow this means:

1. Sign in to your class and click the Students tab.

2. Click Invite.

3. In the Select Students to Invite discourse box, check the cases close to the entirety of the students you wish to invite to the class.

4. Click Invite Students.

Your class list updates to incorporate the students you just invited. The invited students get an email requesting that they join the class. Every student needs to click the connection in the email to join the class.

Note: The students must have an email address having a place with the school's space, for example, yourname@youruniversity.edu. You can't invite individuals outside your school's area.

On the off chance that you have countless students to look over, utilize the Inquiry field at the top to discover the students in your class.

Invite students with the entrance code

To save yourself the hour of welcoming every one of your students, you can have your students assume the liability of welcoming themselves to the class with an uncommon access code.

Here's the secret:

1. Sign in to your class and get the class code on the base left.

2. Give that code to your students through the most helpful strategy, (for example, composing it on your classroom board or remembering it for a gift).

3. Advise your students to go to classroom.google.com, click the, in addition, to sign at the top, and type in the code to join the class.

Note: If, for reasons unknown, you have to incapacitate or reset the entrance code, go to the Stream tab of your class and click the drop-down menu close to the entrance code. Reset doles out another code to the class, crippling the old code. Students need to rejoin the class with the new code. Incapacitate causes it so students can no longer access the class with that code.

Adding materials on your Google Classroom

1. Visit classroom.google.com.

2. Then move straight, click on the class on Classwork.

Then at the top, simply click on **Create** then on **Material**.

See the screenshot below:

1. Put in a title and also a description.

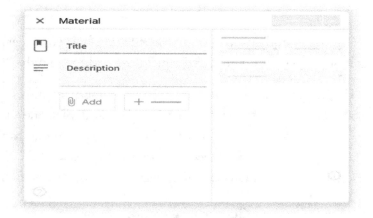

Adding attachments to your Google Classroom

Here you can go ahead and add Google Drive files, documents, links, or YouTube videos to your materials.

If you want to upload a file, all you need to do is to click Attach. Select the file and then click **Upload**.

To attach a Google Drive file:

1. Just click **Drive.**

2. Then select the item and then click **Add.**

Please Note: Assuming you see an error message that you don't have permission to attach a file, then click **Copy**. The classroom makes a copy to attach to the material and saves it to the class Drive folder.

If you want to attach a YouTube video, then click on YouTube and choose an option:

If you want to search for a video to attach:

Follow these simple steps:

A. In the search box, enter keywords and then click Search.

B. Click the video **Add.**

If you want to attach a video link:

A. Then click **the URL.**

B. Just enter the URL and click **Add.**

If you want to attach a link, just click on Link, then enter the URL, and click **Add Link.**

If you want to delete an attachment, all you have to do is click Remove.

Posting to one or more classes on Google Classroom

Under **Form**, just click on the Down arrow then select the class or classes you want to include.

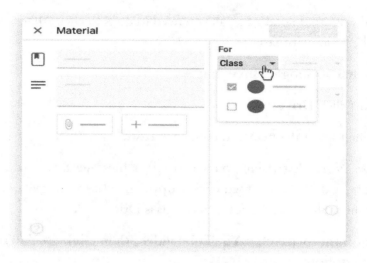

How to invite another teacher to co-teach your class

1. Just visit classroom.google.com.

2. Then go ahead and click the class you want to add co-teachers or groups to.

3. Then at the top of the site, click on the **People**.

Then click on the Invite teachers .

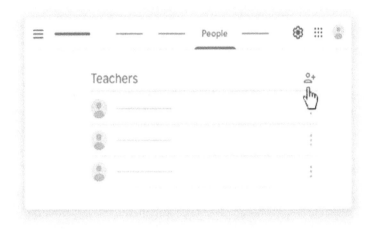

Go ahead and invite separate teachers or a group of them. Go ahead and enter the email address of the teacher or the team.

When you enter text, Google classroom shows some matching addresses that you can choose from.

1. Then on the **search results**, just click a teacher or team.

2. (This is optional) You can invite more teachers or groups, to do that...just repeat the steps 5-6.

3. And finally, click on **Invite**.

To accept an invitation to co-teach a class

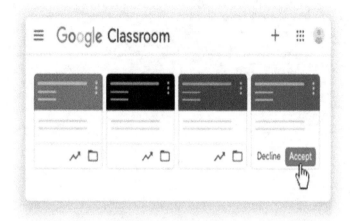

The invited teachers that get an email asking them to co-teach the class. An to join the class, all the invited teacher has to do is to click a link in the email, or sign in to Classroom and click then **Accept** on the class card.

Chapter 12

20 Best Chrome Extensions for Students

egardless of whether you are in school or even in college, the fact is you are Rinvesting a ton of energy utilizing the Google Chrome program. Thus, why not feel free to utilize it viably. What's more, that is the place Chrome Extension comes in.

These are light-weight add-ons that you can add to your program to receive most in return. In this section, we will discuss the absolute best Chrome extensions for students to get the greatest out of their time while perusing the web, concentrating on the web, or in any event, sending assignments through the mail.

Here are the best chrome extensions for students:

1. Google Dictionary

The web is an incredible spot for learning and as a rule, while perusing an article, a post, or even a remark, you run over another word which you have no clue about what it implies. While you can find it on a word reference or open another tab and quest for the word, Google gives a handle little expansion utilizing which you can get the importance of any word just by double-tapping it. Google Dictionary is outstandingly valuable when you are attempting to gain proficiency with another dialect and regardless of whether you aren't, it's a brisk method to look into the significance of words.

2. Grammarly

Grammarly for Chrome resembles your own editor which isn't just fit for recognizing spelling botches yet in addition amending ill-advised language structure. Grammarly works continuously indicating every one of your mistakes as you compose anything and offer recommendations to address them. Like Google Dictionary, it likewise gives implications of words by double-tapping on them, in spite of the fact that it works just on English. Grammarly is a blessing whether you are making a mail to your teacher or making your resume, as it remedies each one of those small botches that may be missed by you and making you look much increasingly professional.

Speedy Tip: Grammarly additionally accompanies a versatile application and supports matching up and backing up of all your work, alongside its editing.

Value: Free ($11.66/month charged every year for Premium)

3. Mercury Reader

Next up on our rundown is Mercury Reader, an augmentation that will improve your perusing experience on the web. With only a tick, Mercury Reader reformats the page, evacuating all the meddlesome advertisements and giving you a smooth perusing experience without all the interruptions. You additionally have the choice of redoing your peruser with content size, text styles, topics and furthermore appointing an alternate way for faster access to Mercury peruser. With Readability being stopped, Mercury peruser is an incredible other option, if worse, for your messiness free perusing on the web.

Speedy tip: If you have a Kindle, there's additionally a component called "Send to Kindle", which sends the delightfully formatted article to your Kindle. That is truly slick!

4. Noisli

Noisli is one of those tools which you had never envisioned you required, yet subsequent to utilizing it you can't simply return. Noisli is a surrounding sound creating tool which offers twelve of foundation seems as though downpour, leaves mumbling, thunder, and background noise a couple, which you can use to support your efficiency or even unwind. What's much cooler is that you can redo each channel as indicated by your taste and once done, you can save it as your own preset to be utilized later. Noisli has been an extraordinary expansion to my armory of Chrome augmentations and I have never thought back.

5. Square and Focus

While the web can be an extraordinary learning place, it tends to divert and considerably progressively negative too. This is the place Block and Focus becomes an integral factor. It is a Chrome expansion that you can use to obstruct certain sites like online life destinations or whichever you like and you won't have the option to get to them for that timeframe. Albeit there is no hope on the off chance that you just don't have the discretion, this augmentation is a decent method to begin.

Fast Tip: Using the settings, you can likewise actualize a Pomodoro clock.

6. PushBullet

PushBullet is an incredible approach to present consistent availability between your PC and your cell phone. When you have the application on your telephone and the augmentation on your Chrome program, you can trade anything between the gadgets like connections, pictures, files, and the widespread clipboard lets you duplicate something on your telephone and glue it on your PC or the other way around. PushBullet comes in extremely helpful on the off chance that you are continually shuffling between your PC and your telephone and increment your profitability by folds.

Value: Free ($4.99/month for Pro)

7. Wolfram Alpha

On the off chance that you are a Science or Engineering student, odds would you say you are have known about Wolfram Alpha; yet did you know, they even have their own Google Chrome augmentation? Alongside the capacity to straightforwardly look on Wolfram Alpha, having the augmentation gives you a clever setting menu which you can use to legitimately feature questions or conditions and look or tackle them. Generally speaking, it is an incredible augmentation to have and comes in extremely helpful on the off chance that you are managing conditions or any sort of calculations.

8. Boomerang for Gmail

Boomerang for Gmail is a magnificent tool going you different controls like booking your sends, napping certain sends, mechanizing follow-up answers, and significantly more, making it an ideal expansion to your Gmail suite. Regardless of whether it's finishing a task at 3 am and booking it for 8 am, or boomeranging(snoozing) a specific mail to be reminded later, Boomerang has you secured. It additionally bolsters read receipts so you know when somebody has really opened or perused your mail.

9. FireShot

FireShot is a screen catching utility like no other accessible on your machine. It is fit for taking screen captures of website pages on your program; at the same time, how is it not quite the same as your framework's screen capture taking tool? All things considered, first of all, FireShot catches just the site page precluding your menu bar and opened tabs, giving a cleaner and progressively professional looking screen capture. The component I like the most about FireShot is it can likewise take an all-encompassing screen capture of the website page, consequently looking till it arrives at the end. Also, also the entire host of choices accessible to which you can change over your screen capture straightforwardly or share them legitimately. I utilize this application at whatever point I am taking a screen capture on Chrome and can't suggest it more.

10. Meeting Buddy

We as a whole have been there when we are examining for an undertaking or reading for a specific point, and the entire program gets overpowered by all the tabs that are opened and in the event that we need to chip away at it following day, we need to either open them from history or bookmark them; generally speaking, it's a problem. Meeting Buddy is a straightforward meeting director utilizing which you can save a "meeting" of your program, for example, all the tabs that were open and later open them just by a solitary snap. This expansion has saved personal time and burden on numerous events and is an absolute necessity have for any student.

11. Pocket

Pocket is a simple method to store and compose different articles, pictures, recordings, and pages from anyplace on the web. When you have the augmentation introduced on your Google Chrome program, and snap on the expansion to save the entire page or right-click on pictures and recordings and Save them to Pocket. You likewise get the alternative of including labels and in this manner keeping your saved things increasingly sorted out. There are additionally cell phone applications that sync every one of your information, so you can get to them from anyplace.

Speedy Tip: For saved articles, Pocket reformats them to an increasingly comprehensible format, like that of Mercury peruser.

12. Force

Force for Chrome is another must-have augmentation to upgrade your Chrome understanding and receive the more in return. Force is a trade for the new tab page in Chrome and accomplishes such a great deal more. Most importantly, it shows another delightful picture ordinarily alongside a moving statement, plan for the day, updates, climate projection in a customizable dashboard. Furthermore, best of all, you don't lose any usefulness of the new tab page, as you can likewise keep your bookmarks and different connections in Momentum. While there is an or more form that offers a further plan for the day mix and more prominent customization, we felt the essential rendition ought to be ideal for most students.

Value: Free ($2.50/month for Plus)

13. Refer to This For Me: Web Citer

In the event that you have ever composed a science report for your venture or an article for a diary, you realize that it is so agonizing to format and oversee references for all the sources which you have utilized in that composition. Enter "Refer to This For Me". Just go to the site page which you need to refer to and click the expansion symbol. The expansion at that point makes an appropriately formatted reference of that website page which you would then be able to reorder in your task. It likewise underpins a bunch of reference referencing styles like Chicago, Harvard, APA, or MLA.

14. Cushion

This expansion is for all the internet-based life dynamic students out there. Support in its center is basic; it permits you to plan every one of your posts much early on the entirety of your preferred web-based life platforms, for example, Facebook, Instagram, and Twitter. The augmentation permits you to share or calendar anything including site pages, pictures, and recordings straightforwardly to your online networking handles. Cradle additionally furnishes you with an examination of every one of your posts and how well they are getting along.

Value: Free ($15/month for Pro)

15. Settle

Spreed is an expansion that causes you speed read through any article or site or even content that you have reordered into the Spreed peruser. The peruser additionally permits a lot of design alternatives, for example, setting the word speed, text dimension, and content shading. On the off chance that you have not ever attempted speed perusing, I'd energetically prescribe you to in any event check out it and perceive the amount you like it. It will build your productivity to process information at a more prominent speed and is extraordinary major expertise to have.

Fast Tip: If you are simply beginning, decline the speed to the one you feel good at and afterward progressively stir your way up.

16. Determination Reader (Text to Speech)

On the off chance that you are lethargic like me, at that point the past augmentation for perusing is most likely isn't for you. With Selection peruser, we have you secured as well, as it basically changes over any content you toss at it to discourse and peruses out the entire content to you. Well that is advantageous! It is additionally amazingly valuable for students experiencing issues in perusing or simply tuning in to something while at the same time accomplishing some other work. While we wish the voice and perusing were somewhat less automated, it gets the activity done quite well.

17. LastPass

Another expansion you may discover helpful is a secret phrase administrator and LastPass tops our proposal list. It is a hearty secret word director that lets you safely store passwords, charge card data, and adjusts through the entirety of your gadgets. It additionally improves online security via naturally producing solid and secure passwords that you don't need to recall them as LastPass carries out the responsibility for you. Obviously, you can see and access all your put away passwords through an "ace secret word" which is the main secret phrase you should recall.

Value: Free ($2/month for Premium)

18. Imagus

Imagus is another of those straightforward tools you never thought you required, yet in the wake of utilizing it, you can't return. Being a Mac client, I was constantly confounded by the way that Google Chrome didn't have Safari's power contact to review a picture, video, or connection. Well with Imagus you can view or see picture or video connects just by drifting your cursor over the connection. This comes in incredibly convenient and you don't any longer need to open another tab just to see a solitary picture.

19. Ears: Bass Boost, EQ Any Audio!

In the event that you are an audiophile or simply tune in to a great deal of music, this next expansion may extravagant you. Ears is a volume promoter and equalizer with plentiful recurrence agents to modify the sound coming out of Chrome. The interface is graphical and exceptionally simple to utilize and you can save all your presets to utilize them later. You can even redo every tab with an alternate preset or diverse setup, which is entirely cool.

Value: Free ($0.99/month for Pro)

20. Nectar

Just a student realizes how close cash can be during those occasions at school and school. So, for the last one, we chose to incorporate an augmentation that can conceivably save you a ton of cash on the off chance that you will in a general shop on the web. In crude terms, Honey is a coupon code supplier for different online retailers yet what makes it shrewd is that it wisely applies the entirety of the coupons accessible on the site and consequently chooses the most limited or best one for you. While outside the US, Honey is to a greater extent a hit or miss with most online retailers; however, on the off chance that you are a student in the US and not utilizing Honey, you are missing out on a ton of free reserve funds!

So, this is our rundown of the best Chrome extensions for students.

Chapter 13

GOOGLE CLASSROOM TIP - Approaches
To Oversee Students Assignments

Alongside guidance and evaluation, assignments form the establishment of the instructing and learning process. They give chances to students to rehearse the aptitudes and apply the information that they have been educated in a strong domain. It likewise enables the teacher to check how well students are learning the material and that they are so near authority.

As a result of the idea of assignments, overseeing them can get feverish. That is the reason its best to utilize a platform like Google Classroom to assist you with overseeing assignments carefully. In the present tip, we will examine 48 different ways that you can utilize the Classroom to oversee student assignments.

Task Status – Effectively check what number of students turned in a task just as what number of assignments have been reviewed by setting off to the Classwork tab and tapping on the title of the task.

Appoint to Numerous Classes – Post a task to different classes by utilizing the "for" drop-down menu while making a task.

Conceptualize – Use Google Docs, Sheets, Slides, or Drawings to conceptualize for class assignments.

Calendar of Due Dates – Connection a Google Calendar with due dates for assignments, tests, and other significant dates into the Classroom.

Check Schoolwork – Classroom makes checking schoolwork simple with a brisk look at the task page. In the event that increasingly nitty-gritty reviewing is required, simply get to the evaluating interface for the task.

Decision Sheets – Give students a decision by the way they exhibit what they know by making a decision board and transferring it as a task. Decision sheets permit students to pick between a few assignments and can be made legitimately in the Classroom, utilizing Google Docs, or with outsider applications.

Co-Show Classes – Welcome others to co-educate in your Classroom. Every teacher can make assignments and post declarations for students.

Make Inquiries Before a Socratic Workshop – Make a task for students to create inquiries before a Socratic class. During the community-oriented procedure, students can take out copy questions.

Detainment Task Sheet – Make a confinement task sheet utilizing Google Docs. The task sheet would then be able to be imparted to the detainment teacher and individual students secretly through the Classroom.

Separate Assignments – Allot work to singular students or gatherings of students in the Classroom.

The separate result – Separate side-effect in the Classroom by giving a test, assortment, or decision or by utilizing a continuum with assignments.

Advanced Portfolios – Students can make computerized arrangement of their work by transferring reports, pictures, curios, and so on to Classroom assignments.

Bearings Report – Use Google Docs to make guidance records for assignments in the Classroom.

Appropriate Student Work/Schoolwork – Use Classroom to disperse student assignments or schoolwork to all students, gatherings of students, or individual students.

Enhance Student Entries – Make elective accommodation alternatives for students through the task tool. For instance, one gathering of students might be required to present a Google Doc while another gathering is required to present a Slides introduction.

Do-Now Exercises – Use Classroom to post Do-Now Exercises.

Draft Assignments – Save posts as drafts until they are prepared for distributing.

Input Before Student Submits – Give criticism to students while their task is as yet a work in progress as opposed to holding up until accommodation. This will enable the student to all the more likely to comprehend task desires.

Get Informed Generally Assignments – Select warning settings to get advised each time a task is turned in late.

Worldwide Classroom – Join forces with global teachers to make a co-encouraging classroom without outskirts where students can deal with community assignments.

Realistic Coordinators – Transfer realistic coordinators for students to work together on assignments and activities.

Gathering Coordinated effort – Dole out different students to a task to make a community-oriented gathering. Give students altering rights to permit them access to a similar archive.

HyperDocs – Make and transfer a hyperdoc as a task.

Connection to Assignments – Make connects to assignments not made in the Classroom.

Connection to Class Blog – Give the connection to a class blog in the Classroom.

Connection to Next Action – Give a connection to the following movement students must finish in the wake of completing a task.

Make a Duplicate for Every Student – Picked "make a duplicate for every student" while transferring task archives to maintain a strategic distance from students sharing one duplicate of the record. At the point when a duplicate for every student is made, Classroom naturally adds every student's name to the archive and saves it to the Classroom folder in Google Drive.

Move to Top/Base – Move late assignments to the highest point of the Classwork feed so students can discover new errands all the more rapidly.

Different File Transfer – Transfer numerous files for a task in one post.

Naming Shows for Assignments – Make a novel naming framework for assignments so they can be handily found in the Classroom folder in Google Drive.

Disconnected Mode – Change settings to permit students to work in disconnected mode if web associations are frail. When a web association is set up, students can transfer assignments to the Classroom.

One Student One Sheet – In Google Sheets, appoint one tab (sheet) per student for the student to finish the task.

One Student One Slide – In Google Slides, appoint one slide to every student to introduce discoveries on a theme or to finish a task.

Compose Student Work – Google Classroom consequently makes calendars and folders in Drive to keep assignments sorted out.

Companion Coaches – Dole out friend guides to help battling students with assignments.

Secure Protection – Google Classroom just permits class individuals to get to assignments. Likewise, it takes out the need to utilize email, which might be less private than the Classroom.

Give Lodging – Furnish facilities to students with incapacities in Google Classroom by permitting additional opportunity to turn in assignments, utilizing content to discourse capacities, and outsider extensions for shaded overlays.

Reorder Assignments by Status – Rather than sorting out assignments by the student's first or last name, arrange them by status to see which students have or have not turned in work.

Reuse Posts – Reuse posts from earlier assignments or from different Classrooms.

See the Procedure – Students don't need to present their assignments for you to see their work. At the point when you picked "make a duplicate for every student" for assignments, every student's work can be found in the reviewing tool, regardless of whether it's not submitted. Teachers can offer remarks and recommendations en route.

Offer Materials – Transfer required materials, for example, the class schedule, rules, strategies, and so on to a Class Assets Module, or transfer task materials inside the task.

Offer Assets – Make an asset list or an asset module for students.

Offer Answers for a Task – Offer answers for a task with a teammate or students after the sum total of what assignments have been turned in.

Quit Rehashing Bearings – By presenting a headings archive on assignments, the need to persistently rehash bearings is reduced, if not disposed of by and large. Remember that a few students will in any case need headings to peruse orally or explained.

Student Work Assortment – Use the Classroom to gather student work from assignments.

Summer Assignments – Make summer assignments for students in the Classroom.

Formats – Make layouts for undertakings, expositions, and other student assignments.

Track Assignments Turned In – Monitor which students turned in assignments by heading off to the reviewing tool.

Chapter 14

What's New in Google Classroom?

he platform has been refreshed a considerable amount since its dispatch, and
TGoogle keeps on introducing new highlights regularly, frequently dependent
on criticism from teachers. For quite a while, users have been lamenting
Google Classroom's absence of grading highlights or a tool for creating
rubrics.

Google tuned in and is rolling out another tool for collecting and grading
work, called Assignments, late in the 2019-2020 school year. Anybody with
access to G Suite for Education can apply to evaluate the Assignments beta
for nothing.

1. Drag and Drop On The Classwork Page

This is a sort of new Classwork page where educators can remain made
with chart their classes. In any case, we comprehend that teachers sort out their
classes explicitly propensities and need extra adaptability in their classroom
tools. So now, you can relocate whole topics and individual Classwork things,
altering them effectively on the page. You can drag a whole point to a particular
zone on the Classwork page, or drag singular things inside—and in—topics.
This accommodation pushed a year earlier on versatile, and now it's the ideal
open entryway for it to hit the web.

2. Invigorated Ux

Directly from now, you'll persistently observe that Classroom has a superior look and sentiments. First on the page, and soon in the Classroom versatile applications. Over the most recent couple of years, we recognizable Google's new material subject with having more consistency across Google things and platforms. Among the changes, you'll see an unyieldingly normal game plan stream—despite another way to deal with oversee shape, covering, iconography, and typography, on both the web and the advantageous application. We're besides making the class code less hard to access and experience so students can without a truly amazing stretch find and join. At long last, we're giving 78 new topics custom portrayals, going from history to math to hairdressing to photography. Eventually, you can re-attempt your Classroom like never before as of now.

3. Refreshed Training and Backing

At last with its new tools and progressively different changes comes the essential for much better help. In the Teacher Social order, you'll find resuscitated records in our First Day of Classroom training with the new course of action and highlights we turned out in 2018. While we're pounding perpetually, we assembled a predominant than whenever in late memory Help Center, got along with our District and thing gathering.

The following are past changes to Google Classroom.

Other/Past Changes to Google Classroom Before 2019-2020 School Year

1. Post Questions

Phan clarifies, "You can present inquiries on your group and permit students to have conversations by reacting to one another's answers (or not, contingent upon the setting you pick). For instance, you could post a video and pose students to answer an inquiry about it, or post an article and request that they compose a passage accordingly."

2. Reuse Assignments

In the event that you reuse educational programs quite a long time after year–or if nothing else reuse archives, there is an update you may like. Phan clarifies, "Presently you can reuse assignments, declarations or inquiries from any of your classes — or any class you co-educate, regardless of whether it's from a year ago or a week ago. When you pick what you'd prefer to duplicate, you'll likewise have the option to make changes before you post or dole out it."

3. Improved Calendar Reconciliation

We love changes that improve the work procedure. "In the next month, Classroom will therefore make a calendar for all of your classes in Google Calendar. All assignments with a due date will be normally added to your gathering calendar and kept awake with the most recent. You'll have the choice to see your calendar from inside Classroom or on Google Calendar, where you can truly incorporate class events like field trips or guest speakers."

4. Knock a post

Staying posts on sites, tweets, or Facebook refreshes has for quite some time been a thing. Presently you can do it on Google Classroom too by moving any post to the top.

5. Due dates discretionary

Undertaking based learning, Self-coordinated learning? Creator ed? On the off chance that you utilize long haul ventures or other due-date-less assignments, you would now be able to make assignments without due dates in Google Classroom.

6. Connect a Google Form to a post

In case you're an aficionado of Google Forms (here's a post on utilizing Google Forms to make a self-evaluated test), this is a change you'll appreciate. Phan clarifies, "Numerous teachers have been utilizing Google Forms as a simple method to relegate a test, test, or study to the class. Coming in the following barely any weeks, teachers and students will before long have the option to append Google Forms from Drive to posts and assignments, and get a connection in Classroom to handily see the appropriate responses."

7. YouTube Usefulness

Love YouTube, yet stressed over stunning content? Google hears you. "Since it in like manner contains content that an organization or school presumably won't consider commendable, a month prior we moved advanced YouTube settings for all Google Applications spaces as an Additional Help. These settings empower Applications overseers to keep the YouTube chronicles detectable for set apart in users, similarly as set apart out users on frameworks supervised by the manager.

Chapter 15

Ways to Utilize Google Classroom

t the point when a task, exercise, or unit doesn't work, include your own
Aremarks or have students include their own input), at that point label it or
save it to an alternate folder for correction.

- ✓ Adjust the educational program to different teachers.

- ✓ Offer information with a professional learning network.

- ✓ Keep tests of model composition for arranging.

- ✓ Label your educational program.

- ✓ Request day by day, week after week, by-semester, or yearly criticism from students and guardians utilizing Google Forms.

- ✓ Offer unknown composing tests with students.

- ✓ See what your assignments resemble from the students' perspective.

- ✓ Flip your classroom. The tools to distribute recordings and offer assignments are center to Google Applications for Training.

- ✓ Impart task standards with students.

- ✓ Let students pose inquiries secretly.

- ✓ Let students make their own computerized arrangement of their preferred work.

- ✓ Make a rundown of endorsed inquire about sources. You can likewise separate this by student, gathering, understanding level, and that's just the beginning.

- ✓ Post a declaration for students, or students and guardians.

- ✓ Plan progressively versatile learning encounters for your students–in higher ed, for instance.

- ✓ Have students outline their own development after some time utilizing Google Sheets.

- ✓ Offer due dates with coaches outside the classroom with an open calendar.

- ✓ Email students separately, or as gatherings. Even better, watch as they speak with each other.

- ✓ Make a test that grades itself utilizing Google Forms.

- ✓ Control file rights (see, alter, duplicate, download) on a file-by-file premise.

- ✓ Have student's clergyman venture-based learning antiquities.

- ✓ As a teacher, you can work together with different teachers (same evaluation by group, same content across grade level).

- ✓ Support advanced citizenship by means of a shared connection that is recorded.

- ✓ Use Google Calendar for due dates, occasions outside the classroom, and other significant "'sequential information.'

- ✓ Discuss carefully with students who might be reluctant to 'talk' with you face to face.

- ✓ Smooth out cross-curricular tasks with different teachers.

- ✓ Total and distribute normally got to sites to ensure everybody has the same access, same archives, same connections, and same information.

- ✓ Vertically-adjust student learning by curating and sharing "milestone" student assignments that reflect the dominance of explicit measures.

- ✓ Empower a typical language by unloading principles and offer area-wide.

- ✓ Urge students to utilize their cell phones for formal learning. By getting to archives, YouTube channels, bunch correspondence, advanced portfolio pieces, and more on a BYOD gadget, students will get an opportunity to consider them to be as some different option from an only for-diversion gadget.

- ✓ Make and distribute 'power gauges' (with students, different teachers, and different schools) for straightforwardness and coordinated effort.

- ✓ Elevate distributed as well as school-to-class communications students with different students, students with different teachers, and teachers with different teachers.

- ✓ Make 'by-need' bunches as classes—dependent on understanding level, for instance.

- ✓ Check which students have gotten to which assignments.

- ✓ Give the student input.

- ✓ Add voice remarks to student composing (this requires an outsider application to do as such).

- ✓ Assist students with making content-explicit YouTube channels.

- ✓ 'Shut circuit distribute' commented on exploring papers as indicated by explicit styles (MLA, APA, and so on.) or other something else 'confounding' work.

- ✓ Make an advanced parking garage''' for questions.

- ✓ Control computerized leave slips.

- ✓ Rather than schoolwork, dole out willful 'exercise extensions' for students. At the point when questions emerge about authority or evaluations, allude to who got to and finished what, when.

- ✓ Make folders of incidental exercise materials. advanced adaptations of writings, and so forth.

- ✓ Appreciate more brilliant conferencing with students and guardians with simple to-get to work, information, composing, input, get to information, etc.

- ✓ Save pdfs or different depictions of advanced assets, in general, got to folders.

- ✓ Make an information divider however with spreadsheets and shading coding.

- ✓ Make sub-work or make-up work simple to get to.

- ✓ Gather information. This can occur in an assortment of ways, from utilizing Google Forms, extraction to Google Sheets, or your own in-house strategy.

- ✓ Give brief criticism for learning.

- ✓ See who's finished what—and when initially.

- ✓ Track when students turn-in work.

- ✓ Since get to is followed, search for designs in student propensities those that get to assignments quickly, those that reliably come back to work, etc. And impart those patterns (namelessly) to students as a method of conveying "best practices in learning" for students who may not in any case think

- ✓ Separate guidance through tiering, gathering, or Sprout's spiraling.

- ✓ Make bunches dependent on preparation, enthusiasm, understanding level, or different variables for instructing and learning.

- ✓ Use Google Forms to survey students, make per user intrigue reviews, and that's only the tip of the iceberg.

- ✓ Model a work referred to page.

- ✓ Make reference sheets.

- ✓ Structure computerized group building exercises.

- ✓ Make a paperless classroom.

- ✓ Offer all-inclusive and as often as possible got to assignments—venture rules, year-long due dates, math formulas, content-region realities, recorded courses of events, and so forth.

Chapter 16

Ways to Motivate Your Students in the Classroom

otivation, truth be told, is one of the fundamental establishments of a Msuccessful classroom. As a teacher, you will never under any circumstance arrive at the objective without propelling your students. Motivation really is certainly not a convoluted term and it is likewise not a troublesome undertaking to persuade your students.

We are experiencing our lives with satisfaction and joy, and agony and distresses since we are persuaded to push ahead. Indeed, now and then in our lives being dismissed and unsettled we stop our desire to proceed onward, however as human instinct, being propelled, we again begin to think to proceed onward. So also, in the vast majority of the cases without being spurred, a student loses want to consider. That is the explanation the students need motivation.

A teacher can't be a fruitful teacher except if s/he realizes how to persuade a student. A fruitful teacher is an individual who knows about the realities and methods on how s/he can make a successful classroom, where the student will partake eagerly. Truth be told, without inspiring your student, you won't have the option to satisfy your sole duty.

There are numerous approaches to spur students in the classroom. Here are probably the best tips to rouse your students in the classroom. Truth be told, such tips on propelling your students will assist you with making your classroom compelling and inventive.

Realize Your Student Well

You should realize your students well. You ought to likewise know their preferences, aversions, proficiency, and lacking. At the point when your students comprehend that you realize them well, they will begin preferring you and uncovering their snags. At that point, it will be simpler for you to persuade your students on the correct way. Except if realizing them well, you probably won't have the option to propel them.

Offer Their Experience

Not all students will share their experiences during the exercise. Some will be occupied with books. Be that as it may, when a few students will examine their experience identified with the exercise, others will be inspired to take an interest effectively. Set up your exercise so that various kinds of students will take an interest excitedly in experience sharing exercise. In such a case, different students likewise get spurred to take an interest in sharing their own encounters. In this manner, you can guarantee a compelling classroom.

Positive Rivalry

The rivalry is, truth be told, a positive method in a classroom. Guarantee positive rivalry. Positive rivalry in bunch work persuades students monstrously. Indeed, even they are set up to deal with bunch work, which will acquire an extraordinary advantage in their professional life too. It is no denying actuality that positive rivalry triggers inspiration among your students in the classroom.

Incredible Audience

Listen cautiously to what your student needs to communicate. Value their feels and considerations. Find a way to sift through the challenges they are grumbling about. Be an incredible audience. They will begin enjoying you as you hear them out with legitimate consideration. Along these lines, you can gain their trust. Presently, isn't it simple to persuade them? On the off chance that you need your students ought to hear you out, you should hear them out first.

Trust Them and Give Them Duty

Give your students a duty. Dole out them some classroom action. They will include devotion without a doubt. Once more, in such a case, a few students will likewise figure out how to perform obligations. At the point when you will give them obligations, a trust inside themselves will develop and they will begin accepting that they are significant since they are getting an incentive from you. Along these lines, they will be persuaded to take part effectively in the classroom. At the point when you are confiding in them, consequently, they will confide in you moreover.

Express Your Fervor

Express your fervor in the classroom during an exercise while they are satisfying their obligations. Offer your fervor on their incredible performance. Again, express your positive fervor additionally when another thought is presented by any student. Your demeanor of energy will trigger inspiration for them.

Keep Record

Set up a record for you. Record every one of your student's performance. At the point when you locate that a specific student is improving, talk about the student on the improvement. Demonstrate the record to the student. Reward and value the student before the classroom. Indeed, even offer the enhancements with the guardians. At the point when a student finds that you care for that student as you are talking about from your record, the student gets roused.

Positive Input

At the point when a student isn't progressing admirably, give positive criticism. Give additional opportunity if conceivable. Resemble a companion and attempt to comprehend the instance of such a horrible showing. Energize the student spurring that next time s/he can undoubtedly improve as s/he was unable to see how to perform well in this subject with the best possible information and method.

Guess what? Your positive criticism can change numerous lives. Cautiously take a gander at the most fragile students in your classroom, you will clearly get numerous positive characteristics. Inform them about such incredible characteristics they are having. Actually, value them, which consequently will propel them essentially.

A Classroom Blog

On the off chance that you're a teacher, at that point, you in all probability have followed a blog or two to gain some new useful knowledge. Sites are a pleasant method to pick up information and information through the methods for innovation. It's likewise an extraordinary tool to use in the classroom to help rouse students to learn. Teachers love them since they offer their students a chance to peruse, compose, and be inventive.

Students love them and discover them profoundly propelling in light of the fact that their friends get the chance to perceive what they compose on the web. The extraordinary thing about a classroom blog is the posts can be as short or long as you can imagine. They can likewise be gotten to from anyplace that you can interface with the web.

Numerous teachers use them in a wide range of ways, from having students set up their very own blog and use it to distribute their composition, to utilizing it as a student portfolio, or as an information center point. However, you choose to utilize it, it will be an extraordinary help for your students.

Mapping Innovation

Mapping innovation, or GPS innovation, is another extraordinary tech tool to use in the classroom to inspire students. This kind of innovation can know where you are at some random second, which can be many good times for students. On the off chance that you have a cell phone or an iWatch, you'll have a GPS tracker following all your minutes, which is an extraordinary route for students to investigate the world and earth around them.

A pleasant way that you can utilize this innovation in your classroom is to go on the web and utilize a mapping tool like Google Earth. Goggle Earth enables students to see where they are on the planet or where they need to go. Teachers are utilizing this program to carry their geology lessons to an unheard-of level. They have students go on an online forager chase looking for wells of lava, little nations they may have never known about, or even quest for mansions. The thoughts are perpetual.

Another great method to keep students roused is to Geo-store. Geo-reserving with students includes a multistep puzzle a lot of like a fortune chase. It's an extraordinary method to show students different abilities, for example, critical thinking and math. Ultimately, Map My Run is an extraordinary mapping application that shows students the separation they went on a field outing or how far they strolled around the school. Teachers like to combine their students together and give them a tablet so they can follow themselves utilizing the application. These mapping advancements are an extraordinary, intelligent approach to keep students persuaded in what they are realizing in school.

Attempt to submerge your students in innovation as much as possible, not just in light of the fact that it's an extraordinary helper for them, but since the future, we are living in. Keep awake-to-date on all the most recent in instructive advancements, with the goal that your students will get the most present training that will assist them with prevailing in the computerized universe of today.

Conclusion

lassroom significantly supplements your writing board showing aptitudes as Ca teacher: you can dole out schoolwork, check tutorials, make tests, quizzes, and grade your students. And furthermore, it improves your learning abilities as a student. Isn't that awesome?

You can go ahead and start making use of this amazing Google Classroom platform. Did you find this guide useful? Share your experience in the review section.

Thanks for investing in this book. I'm sure you have learned a few things about Google Classroom and how you can start benefiting with it. So, if you enjoyed reading this guide.

If you find this book useful and want to encourage me to produce more guides like this, kindly leave an honest review on Amazon.

The End.

CPSIA information can be obtained
at www.ICGtesting.com
Printed in the USA
LVHW080248141120
671604LV00002B/2

9 781513 668857